The Sleeping Generation: Awakening a Lukewarm World to Redemption, Purification, and Eternal Reality

Servant of CHRIST

Disclaimer

This book is a work of spiritual and theological reflection. While it draws extensively from Sacred Scripture and the historic Christian tradition, it is not intended as a substitute for pastoral counsel, sacramental life, or personal spiritual direction. Readers are encouraged to seek guidance appropriate to their individual circumstances.

Library of Congress Control Number (LCCN): 2026900834

Scripture Acknowledgements

Unless otherwise noted, Scripture quotations in this book are taken from the Revised Standard Version, Catholic Edition (RSV-CE).
Copyright © 1966, 2006 by the Division of Christian Education of the National Council of the Churches of Christ in the United States of America. Used by permission. All rights reserved.

Where alternate traditional phrasing appears, citations reflect theological continuity rather than textual variance.

Doctrinal Note

This work draws upon Sacred Scripture and the historic Christian tradition, with particular resonance within Catholic theology, while remaining accessible to all Christians willing to engage seriously with the call to sanctification, vigilance, and faith lived in response to grace.

Publication Information

ISBN: 979-8-9945326-3-8
Printed in the United States of America

CONTENTS

HOW TO READ THIS BOOK

This book was not written for hurried reading or casual reflection. It was written for those who sense—perhaps quietly, perhaps uneasily—that something essential is at stake in their spiritual life that deserves more than surface attention.

It is intended for thoughtful readers who desire depth rather than reassurance; for believers seeking a faith that engages the whole person— mind, will, and heart; for Christians who have grown dissatisfied with a spirituality that comforts without transforming; and for anyone willing to examine their life honestly in the light of eternity.

What follows does not offer quick answers or easy encouragement. It asks the reader to slow down, to listen carefully, and to consider the weight of choices that are often postponed or softened in modern religious conversation. It speaks plainly about grace and freedom, mercy and judgment, purification and hope— not to unsettle those who seek sincerely, but to awaken those who are ready to hear.

This is not a casual devotional. It does not aim to be read quickly or set aside easily. That is not a deficiency, but a deliberate strength. The truths considered here require patience, reflection, and interior honesty. They are not new, but they are often neglected.

If you are seeking a book that affirms without challenging, this may not be the one. But if you are seeking a faith that is alive, demanding, and worthy of your full response—one that takes both God's mercy and your freedom seriously—then you are invited to continue.

This book does not claim to resolve every mystery. It seeks instead to clarify responsibility, restore reverence, and encourage a life lived awake before God.

The invitation it offers is simple, but not easy: to live deliberately, to love honestly, and to walk in the light while there is still time.

A PASTORAL EXHORTATION TO THE CHRISTIAN READER

This book speaks plainly about eternity, responsibility, and response. It does so intentionally. Yet it is important to say clearly what this work is not meant to do.

It is not written to provoke fear in those who sincerely desire God. It is not written to unsettle tender consciences or to burden souls already striving to love Him. It is not written to suggest that anxiety, struggle, or weakness are signs of rejection.

On the contrary, Scripture consistently reveals that the desire for God itself is already the work of grace. Those who fear being separated from Him, who grieve over sin, who long for holiness—even imperfectly—are not the souls described as resisting grace. Concern for one's spiritual state is not evidence of abandonment, but often evidence of awakening.

This book addresses not fragile faith, but presumption; not weakness, but refusal; not sincere struggle, but postponed surrender. It speaks to the danger of delay, not to the reality of imperfection. It warns against mistaking God's patience for permission, not against trusting His mercy. If, while reading, you find yourself moved toward repentance, humility, or deeper trust in God, do not conclude that you are condemned. Such movements are signs that grace is at work. The call to awaken is not a threat to those who love God; it is an invitation meant to preserve them.

God does not ask for fear. He asks for honesty. He does not demand perfection achieved alone. He offers sanctification completed by grace. And He does not withdraw mercy from those who seek Him. Read attentively. Read slowly. Read with prayer. But do not read with despair. As long as the heart still turns toward God—even quietly, even imperfectly—hope remains very much alive.

INTRODUCTION

AWAKE, O SLEEPER

"Awake, O sleeper, and arise from the dead, and Christ shall give you light." (Ephesians 5:14)

We are not living in an age that hates God.
We are living in an age that delays Him.

This generation still believes, still prays, still speaks the language of faith. Yet something essential has gone quiet. Eternity has become distant. Urgency has faded. Holiness is postponed. Grace is assumed. Tomorrow feels guaranteed. This is not rebellion; it is sleep. Scripture warns that sleep is more dangerous than opposition, because it dulls the soul while convincing it that all is well. The greatest threat to the spiritual life today is not persecution or unbelief, but postponement—the quiet decision to take God seriously later. Yet Saint Paul speaks with clarity: now is the time. Not when life slows down. Not when circumstances improve. Not when we feel ready. 'Now is the acceptable time; now is the day of salvation' (2 Corinthians 6:2)

This book is written because "later" is an illusion. It is written to awaken those who sense—perhaps uncomfortably—that faith has become familiar but not transformative, sincere but not surrendered, orthodox but not urgent. It is written for those who love God, yet know they have been holding part of themselves back. These pages will not speculate, sensationalize, or flatter. They will speak honestly about mercy, purification, resistance, awakening, and eternal meaning. They will confront delay, not to condemn, but to call.

Because God is patient—but He is not passive.
Because grace invites—but it also demands response.
Because nothing unclean enters heaven, and nothing done in love is ever lost.

If you are reading this, the door is still open. The light is still offered. The call is still being spoken.

The night is far gone.
The day is at hand.

CHAPTER ONE
A GENERATION ASLEEP WHILE ETERNITY WATCHES

S AINT PAUL ONCE WROTE WORDS THAT SHOULD make every believer pause: "It is full time now for you to wake from sleep" (Romans 13:11). He was not speaking to pagans or skeptics. He was addressing Christians—people who already believed. That alone reveals a sobering truth: it is possible to know Christ and still drift into spiritual sleep. Paul continues by reminding them why urgency matters. Salvation, he says, is nearer now than when they first believed; the night is far gone, and the day is at hand (Romans 13:11–12). Time is moving, whether we are attentive or not. Eternity is not static. Every passing day draws us closer to an encounter we cannot delay or reschedule.

Spiritual sleep does not announce itself as rebellion. It rarely feels dangerous. More often, it feels comfortable. Life appears orderly. Responsibilities are met. Faith is acknowledged. And because nothing seems broken, the soul assumes it is awake. But Scripture warns that belief without vigilance slowly decays into complacency. Jesus Himself illustrated this danger when He spoke of the ten maidens waiting for the bridegroom. All ten carried lamps. All ten expected His arrival. And all ten fell asleep as time passed. Yet only five were prepared when the moment came (Matthew 25:1–5). The tragedy was not that they slept, but that some slept without oil. Expectation without preparation proved fatal. This parable dismantles a modern assumption—that belief automatically equals readiness. Jesus never taught that proximity to religious things guarantees intimacy with God. In fact, He warned that many who call Him "Lord" will be shocked at the final judgment. Some will point to works done in His name—

1

prophecies, miracles, public ministry—yet hear the devastating words, "I never knew you" (Matthew 7:21–23). Activity had replaced obedience. Familiarity had replaced surrender. Spiritual sleep allows this substitution to happen gradually. The soul begins to rely on religious identity instead of conversion. Scripture is known, but not obeyed. Prayer is practiced, but not prioritized. Sin is no longer confronted; it is negotiated. Repentance is postponed because "there is still time."

Jesus asks a question that exposes the illusion beneath spiritual delay: "What will it profit a man, if he gains the whole world and forfeits his life?" (Matthew 16:26). This is not a philosophical question. It is a personal one. Every life is an exchange. Every choice trades something eternal for something temporary—or vice versa. Ecclesiastes speaks bluntly about what happens when eternity is removed from the center of life. After surveying human achievement, success, labor, and pleasure, it concludes that everything done under the sun becomes "vanity and a striving after wind" (Ecclesiastes 1:14). Without God, even accomplishment becomes empty. Without eternity, even abundance leaves the soul restless.

One of the reasons spiritual sleep spreads so easily is that it often grows out of distraction rather than defiance. Jesus warned that the days preceding judgment would resemble the days of Noah. People would be eating, drinking, marrying, and planning for the future right up until the flood arrived (Matthew 24:37–39). Their destruction came not because they were unusually wicked, but because they were unaware. Distracted. Unrepentant. They assumed continuity.

Many today mistake God's patience for God's approval. Because judgment does not arrive immediately, the heart begins to believe it never will. Saint Peter corrects this misunderstanding directly: the Lord is not slow in keeping His promise, but is patient, desiring that all should reach repentance (2 Peter 3:9). His delay is mercy, not indifference. His patience is an invitation, not a guarantee of endless postponement. When mercy is misunderstood, delay becomes habitual. And habitual delay slowly hardens the heart. While human hearts drift, heaven remains fully awake. Scripture reminds us that "we must all appear before the judgment seat of Christ" to receive according to what has been done in the body, whether good or evil (2 Corinthians 5:10). No life is overlooked. No decision is insignificant. Eternity watches even when the soul forgets. That is why Saint Paul

2

repeatedly calls believers to awaken, issuing the command plainly: "Awake, O sleeper, and arise from the dead, and Christ shall give you light" (Ephesians 5:14). This awakening is not emotional excitement. It is moral clarity. It is the recovery of reverence. Scripture teaches that "the fear of the Lord is the beginning of wisdom" (Proverbs 9:10). Where reverence fades, wisdom collapses. And where wisdom collapses, spiritual sleep deepens. Without reverence, grace is treated casually. Without reverence, repentance is delayed. Without reverence, eternity loses its weight. Even Jesus wept over a people who were not openly rebellious but spiritually blind. Looking over Jerusalem, He lamented that they did not recognize "the things that make for peace," and that those things were now hidden from their eyes (Luke 19:42). Blindness is not always willful rejection, sometimes it is the result of prolonged inattention.

This chapter is not written to accuse, but to interrupt. God does not call His people to awaken because He delights in fear. He calls them because sleep leads to loss, and He desires that none be lost. Jesus Himself urged vigilance when He warned, "Watch therefore, for you do not know on what day your Lord is coming" (Matthew 24:42). Watchfulness is not anxiety. It is honesty. It is living with eternity in view. It is allowing truth to shape daily decisions instead of postponing obedience until later. This generation is not beyond hope. But it is vulnerable. It lives as though time were owned rather than entrusted, as though tomorrow were guaranteed, and as though grace could always be accessed later. The Gospel does not support that confidence. It insists that now is the moment of response, now is the day of salvation, and now is the time to wake. Everything that follows in this book depends on this first movement of the soul. There can be no repentance without awareness, no holiness without urgency, and no preparation without vigilance.

Eternity is watching. Heaven is calling. And the night is far gone.

Closing Prayer

Lord God,

You who never sleep nor slumber,
we stand before You aware of how easily our hearts drift into restlessness

disguised as peace,
and comfort mistaken for faithfulness.

Awaken us from every form of spiritual sleep.
Where we have grown inattentive, restore our vigilance.
Where we have delayed obedience, grant us courage to respond now.
Where we have confused Your patience with permission, give us clarity
and reverence.

Teach us to live with eternity in view.
Order our loves rightly, that we may desire You above all things.
Free us from the illusion that time belongs to us
and remind us that every day is entrusted, not guaranteed.

Give us the grace to watch without fear,
to repent without despair,
and to walk in the light while it is still day.

Let Your Spirit disturb what has grown too comfortable,
heal what has grown numb,
and illumine what has grown dim.

May we not be found asleep when You call,
but awake, attentive, and ready—
living not for what passes away,
but for what endures forever.

We ask this through Christ our Lord.

Amen.

CHAPTER TWO
TOMORROW IS NOT PROMISED: DELAY AS DISGUISED DISOBEDIENCE

IF SPIRITUAL SLEEP IS THE CONDITION THAT allows a generation to drift, delay is the habit that keeps it asleep. Delay rarely presents itself as defiance. It arrives quietly, clothed in reasonableness. It whispers that obedience can wait, that repentance can be scheduled, that urgency is unnecessary. In doing so, it trains the heart to live as though time were guaranteed and grace were endlessly accessible. Delay is never neutral.

From beginning to end, God calls His people to respond today, because time is fragile and opportunity fleeting. Wisdom cautions plainly, "Do not boast about tomorrow, for you do not know what a day may bring" (Proverbs 27:1). Tomorrow itself is not condemned. Presumption is. When repentance, forgiveness, or surrender is postponed to an imagined future, authority is subtly shifted from God to time. Jesus exposed this illusion through a parable that feels uncomfortably familiar. A man enjoyed abundant success and planned for long-term ease. He told himself that he had many years to relax, eat, drink, and enjoy life. His plans were logical, responsible, and widely admired. Yet God interrupted that confidence with a single sentence: "Fool! This night your soul is required of you; and the things you have prepared, whose will they be?" (Luke 12:20). Jesus concluded that this is the fate of anyone who stores up treasure for himself but is not rich toward God (Luke 12:21). The man was not condemned for planning; he was condemned for assuming that his soul was secure simply because his future appeared stable. Delay thrives in comfort. When life

5

feels predictable, urgency fades. The heart begins to assume there will always be time later—later to repent, later to reconcile, later to obey.

Yet Scripture repeatedly dismantles this confidence. Saint James confronts those who speak confidently about tomorrow and reminds them that they do not know what tomorrow will bring. He asks, "What is your life?" and answers that it is a mist that appears for a little time and then vanishes (James 4:14). Planning without humility becomes arrogance when it assumes control over time that belongs to God alone. This is the moment when delay crosses from weakness into disobedience. When God has spoken clearly, postponement is not neutral. The Letter to the Hebrews warns believers directly, "Today, when you hear his voice, do not harden your hearts" (Hebrews 3:15). The hardening of the heart does not usually occur through dramatic rebellion. It occurs through repeated delay. Each postponed response makes the next one easier to ignore. The Old Testament gives us a sobering illustration in King Saul. Saul did not reject God outright. He obeyed selectively. Commanded to destroy the Amalekites completely, he spared what he judged valuable and destroyed what seemed worthless (1 Samuel 15:9). When confronted, Saul defended himself with religious language, claiming that the spared goods were intended for sacrifice. Samuel's response exposes the heart of the issue: "To obey is better than sacrifice, and to listen than the fat of rams" (1 Samuel 15:22). Saul's downfall began not with rebellion, but with delayed and partial obedience.

Procrastination often disguises itself as discernment. Many tell themselves they are waiting for clarity, emotional readiness, or a better season. Yet Scripture reveals that God has already spoken clearly about many things. Repentance, forgiveness, humility, reconciliation, prayer, and holiness are not ambiguous commands. Delaying obedience in these areas is not wisdom; it is resistance. Jesus addressed this directly when people attempted to follow Him on their own timeline. To one who wanted to delay discipleship until after burying his father, Jesus replied, "Leave the dead to bury their own dead; but as for you, go and proclaim the kingdom of God" (Luke 9:60). To another who wanted first to say farewell, He said, "No one who puts his hand to the plow and looks back is fit for the kingdom of God" (Luke 9:62). These words unsettle us because they dismantle the idea that obedience can be negotiated around personal convenience. Delayed repentance is especially dangerous because it creates the illusion of control over grace. Paul warns believers not to be deceived, reminding them that the unrighteous will not inherit the kingdom of God (1 Corinthians 6:9). The deception often lies not in denying sin, but in planning to repent later. Repentance that is always future is repentance that never becomes real. Paul's urgency is unmistakable when he writes, "Behold, now is the favorable time; behold, now is the day of salvation" (2 Corinthians 6:2). Grace is not stored for future use. It is offered in the present moment. Obedience can only occur now. Yesterday is gone, and tomorrow is uncertain.

Scripture also warns that persistent delay reshapes the soul. The longer obedience is postponed, the quieter conviction becomes. What once stirred urgency fades into background noise. Hebrews cautions that deliberate sin after receiving the knowledge of the truth leads not to safety, but to fearful judgment (Hebrews 10:26–27). This is not because God's mercy is small, but because presumed repentance is not repentance at all. Jesus describes grace as a door that must be opened while the knocking continues: "Behold, I stand at the door and knock. If anyone hears my voice and opens the door, I will come in" (Revelation 3:20). Delay risks silence—not because God stops loving, but because the heart becomes trained not to respond. Over time, procrastination becomes a way of life. Each delayed "yes" strengthens the habit of refusal. Each postponed confession dulls the conscience. Each deferred act of obedience trains the soul to believe that God's commands are negotiable. Eventually, intention replaces surrender, and desire replaces action.

Jesus exposes this contradiction with a piercing question: "Why do you call me 'Lord, Lord,' and not do what I tell you?" (Luke 6:46). Lordship cannot coexist with habitual delay. To confess Christ as Lord while postponing obedience is to empty the confession of its meaning. Each postponed repentance creates unfinished business within the soul. God does not overlook this unfinished work—not because He is harsh, but because He is faithful. Love does not abandon what is incomplete. Truth does not ignore what remains unresolved. The New Testament insists that God, in His mercy, will complete the work He begins. Saint Paul reminds us that "He who began a good work in you will bring it to completion" (Philippians 1:6). The question is not whether the work will be completed, but how. What we willingly surrender now through repentance and

7

obedience, God heals gently. What we stubbornly delay, He must purify more painfully. This is the sober reality this generation often avoids: delayed surrender does not eliminate purification; it postpones it. What grace invites us to address freely in this life must still be addressed before we can stand fully in the presence of a Holy God. Scripture is clear that "nothing unclean shall enter" the kingdom of heaven (Revelation 21:27). God's mercy does not bypass this truth—it fulfills it. And so the journey does not end with delay; it moves toward purification. If obedience is postponed, purification remains. If surrender is delayed, refinement still awaits. The soul God begins work on will be made ready—either through willing repentance now, or through merciful but painful purification later.

The call remains as direct now as it was centuries ago: "Choose this day whom you will serve" (Joshua 24:15). Tomorrow is not promised. Grace is offered now. Obedience is required now. The soul that responds today escapes the tragedy of delayed surrender and steps into the freedom that only obedience can bring.

Closing Prayer

Lord God,

You who speak in the present moment,
we confess how easily we postpone what You ask of us.
We tell ourselves there will be time later— later to repent, later to obey,
later to surrender— as though tomorrow were ours to command.

Forgive us for the delays we have justified
and the obedience we have negotiated.
Where we have replaced trust with planning,
and surrender with intention,
bring us back to truth.

Teach us to hear Your voice today
and not harden our hearts.

Give us the courage to respond while grace is offered,
to open the door while You still knock,
to say yes without condition or excuse.

Free us from the illusion that repentance can be stored for later use.
Heal what we are willing to surrender now,
so that it need not be purified through pain later.
Train our hearts to love obedience
not as loss, but as freedom.

Lord, we choose this day whom we will serve.
Not tomorrow.
Not when life is quieter.
Not when we feel ready.

But Today.

Complete in us the work You have begun,
according to Your mercy and Your truth,
that we may stand before You
awake, responsive, and made ready.

We ask this through Christ our Lord.

Amen.

CHAPTER THREE
NOTHING UNCLEAN SHALL ENTER HEAVEN

THE NEW TESTAMENT DOES NOT SPEAK AMBIGUOUSLY about heaven. It describes it not only as a place of joy, but as a realm of perfect holiness. At the close of Revelation—after mercy has been fully proclaimed and the Lamb's victory revealed—the vision allows no ambiguity: nothing unclean shall enter, nor anyone who practices falsehood, but only those whose names are written in the Lamb's book of life (Revelation 21:27). This is not a threat. It is a description of reality.

The modern mind recoils at this idea. We are uncomfortable with anything that sounds like exclusion, refinement, or purification. We prefer instant arrival, unconditional acceptance, and immediate rest. Yet the Gospel never presents heaven as a casual destination. It presents heaven as the fullness of God's presence—and the presence of God is not neutral. It is Holy. And holiness does not coexist with disorder. This truth confronts our generation at a vulnerable point. We have grown accustomed to thinking of forgiveness as the end of the story. Once forgiven, we assume the matter is settled. But Scripture makes a careful distinction between forgiveness and purification. Forgiveness removes guilt. Purification removes attachment. Forgiveness reconciles the soul to God. Purification prepares the soul to dwell with Him.

From the beginning, God reveals Himself not only as merciful, but as Holy. When the prophet Isaiah is granted a vision of heaven, he does not encounter warmth or reassurance first. He encounters holiness so overwhelming that the seraphim cry out unceasingly that the Lord of hosts

11

is Holy, and the whole earth is full of His glory (Isaiah 6:3). The response this vision provokes in Isaiah is not confidence, but collapse. He cries out that he is lost, a man of unclean lips dwelling among a people of unclean lips, having seen the King, the Lord of hosts (Isaiah 6:5). This moment is instructive. Isaiah is already chosen by God. He is already a prophet. Yet in the presence of divine holiness, he becomes acutely aware of what still needs to be purified. Only after a seraph touches his lips with a burning coal and declares his guilt removed does Isaiah stand ready to answer God's call (Isaiah 6:6–7). Holiness does not humiliate Isaiah; it heals him. But the healing involves fire. The Letter to the Hebrews exhorts believers to strive for peace with everyone and for the holiness without which no one will see the Lord (Hebrews 12:14). This is not metaphor. It is not exaggeration. Without holiness, vision of God is impossible. God does not adjust heaven to accommodate our disorder; He removes the disorder so that we may endure heaven. What grace invites us to surrender freely in this life, God must still remove before eternal communion is possible.

This raises an unavoidable question. If holiness is required to see God, and if most believers die still imperfect—how does God complete the work He has begun? (as written by Saint Paul in Philippians 1:6). The short answer is completion implies process. God does not abandon the soul in an unfinished state. He finishes what remains incomplete. This finishing is not condemnation; it is mercy refusing to leave the soul half-healed. Saint Paul gives a concrete image of this completion when he describes the testing of each person's work. He explains that some build on the foundation of Christ with lasting material, while others build with what cannot endure. On the day of judgment, each work will be revealed by fire. If the work survives, the person receives a reward. If the work is burned up, the person suffers loss, yet is saved—but only as through fire (1 Corinthians 3:12–15). This passage is striking in its balance. The person is saved. Their foundation remains Christ. Yet something in them cannot remain. Fire removes what does not belong in eternity. The soul is preserved; the disorder is not. Jesus Himself affirms the absolute standard of heaven when He commands His followers to be perfect as their heavenly Father is perfect (Matthew 5:48). This command would be cruel if God did not also provide the means to fulfill it. God does not demand perfection and then abandon the soul to failure. He perfects what He commands—either through cooperation now, or through purification later. This generation often assumes that death instantly resolves all interior disorder. The Church never teaches this. Instead, it teaches continuity. What remains unfinished in the soul does not disappear at death; it must be healed. Purification is not a contradiction of mercy; it is mercy brought to completion. Mercy doesn't lower God's standard; it raises the soul. This is why Jesus speaks of forgiveness extending beyond this life when He says that certain sins will not be forgiven either in this age or in the age to come (Matthew 12:32). The statement holds only if forgiveness and purification can occur beyond death. This teaching is not meant to encourage delay. It is meant to expose its cost. Purification, though merciful, is not painless. Scripture consistently uses the image of fire to describe it. The prophet Malachi asks who can endure the day of the Lord's coming, for He is like a refiner's fire and like fullers' soap, sitting as a refiner and purifier (Malachi 3:2–3). Refining fire does not destroy what is precious. It removes what does not belong. But the process is intense.

This is why we are urged toward sanctification now. Saint Peter exhorts believers not to return to former passions, but to be holy in all their conduct, because God Himself is Holy (1 Peter 1:14–16). Holiness is not an optional enhancement to salvation. It is its fulfillment. It is precisely this readiness that Jesus addresses in the parable of the wedding feast. A man is invited and enters the hall, yet he lacks the wedding garment. When questioned, he has no answer (Matthew 22:11–12). Invitation alone was not enough; preparation was required. Forgiveness opened the door, but purification prepared the guest. This chapter therefore confronts a dangerous misconception—that salvation is merely escape from punishment. The Gospel presents salvation instead as restoration to holiness. Every confession, every act of humility, every surrender to grace removes what cannot enter heaven. The biblical promise remains: if we confess our sins, God is faithful and just not only to forgive, but to cleanse us from all unrighteousness (1 John 1:9).

Purification begins now, not only beyond this life. God has always used suffering, testing, and trial to awaken, refine, and prepare His people. What some souls encounter after death through purification (in purgatory), others are confronted with in life through tribulation. In both cases, the purpose is the same: to separate what belongs to God from what does not.

Purgatory: Purified by Love

Purgatory does not offer a second opportunity to choose God. This life is where the soul's direction is decided. "It is appointed for men to die once, and after that comes judgment" (Hebrews 9:27). Choice belongs to time. After death, the will is fixed. What purgatory addresses is not decision, but completion. Often, at funerals, departed loved ones are spoken of as already at rest, as though the work of sanctification were complete. The Church does not teach this. Instead, it consistently reveals continuity between the spiritual state formed on earth and the soul's condition after death. What grace begins in this life, God completes. Purgatory, then, is not opposed to Christ's redemption. It applies it fully. The cross does not merely pardon; it heals.

This is where modern misunderstandings arise. Many imagine purgatory as a harsh holding cell, a place of anger rather than love. Scripture presents something far more intimate. The suffering of purification is not despair, but longing. It is the pain of proximity to God without yet being able to embrace Him fully. The closer the soul draws to divine holiness, the more acutely it perceives what must still be healed. Purgatory is mercy, not cruelty. God refuses to abandon His children in an unfinished state. The alternative to purification would not be comfort, but exclusion. Without purification, heaven would be unbearable to a disordered soul. Love completes what forgiveness begins. Yet this mercy should never be mistaken for convenience. Saint Paul speaks of real loss. Jesus warns that every careless word will be accounted for (Matthew 12:36). Time matters. Choices matter. Delays matter. What is not healed now must be healed later, but without the freedom to merit, serve, or love others through it. This is why the doctrine of purgatory is not meant to encourage delay, but to expose its cost. Souls habituated to delay often reduce purgatory to a safety net, as though postponed holiness carried no cost. Yet the Church's teachings give no such comfort. It speaks soberly of the cost of procrastination. Purification in purgatory is not the worst outcome— eternal loss is. God completes only the work the heart allows Him to begin while there is still time. Saint Paul therefore urges believers to cooperate with purification now. "Work out your own salvation with fear and trembling; for God is at work in you, both to will and to work for his good pleasure" (Philippians 2:12–13). This is not anxiety, but reverence. Salvation is not casual. Grace demands response.

Saint John connects hope directly to purification when he writes that those who hope to see God purify themselves now, as God is pure (1 John 3:2–3). Hope does not postpone holiness; it accelerates it. Those who truly desire heaven do not delay becoming fit for it. The Saints understood this well. Saint Paul confessed openly that he had not yet attained perfection, but that he pressed on because Christ had made him His own (Philippians 3:12). Pressing on implies effort, urgency, and intentional cooperation with grace. Saint John promises that if we walk in the light, the blood of Jesus cleanses us from all sin (1 John 1:7). We must all hear this clearly: holiness delayed is purification intensified. Grace resisted is mercy deferred. Refining fire heals, but it also exposes the cost of delay.

Closing Prayer

Holy God,

You who are light without shadow
and love without compromise,
we stand before You aware that Your presence is not merely comforting,
but sanctifying.

Cleanse us of what cannot endure Your holiness.
Reveal gently what remains disordered within us,
not to condemn, but to heal.
Where we have mistaken forgiveness for completion,
teach us the grace of purification.
Where we have delayed surrender,
give us courage to yield now.

Do not allow us to cling to what cannot enter Your kingdom.
Refine our hearts while there is still time,
so that the fire of Your love may heal rather than wound.
Free us from the illusion that holiness can be postponed
without cost.

Grant us a holy impatience with our own complacency
and a deeper desire for You than for comfort.
Let hope draw us toward purity,
and love hasten our cooperation with grace.

Finish in us the work You have begun,
according to Your mercy and Your truth,
that we may one day behold You face to face—
not as strangers to holiness,
but as children made ready by love.

We ask this through Christ our Lord.

Amen.

CHAPTER FOUR

LUKEWARMNESS AND THE COST OF INDECISION

I F PURGATORY REVEALS THE MERCY OF A GOD who refuses to abandon unfinished souls, lukewarmness reveals the tragedy of souls who resist that mercy while time still remains. Lukewarmness is not open rebellion. It is a settled compromise. It allows faith to exist without urgency, obedience without sacrifice, and religion without transformation. It clings to God enough to feel safe, yet resists Him enough to avoid change. This condition is especially dangerous because it convinces the soul that nothing is wrong while everything essential remains incomplete. Jesus warns more sharply against lukewarmness than against acknowledged sin, not because He despises weakness, but because lukewarmness refuses repentance and therefore resists healing. It neither flees God nor falls before Him. It remains comfortably distant—close enough to avoid fear, far enough to avoid fire.

The same love that purifies souls after death confronts lukewarm hearts in this life. God's fire does not disappear; it approaches. It presses, exposes, and invites. When welcomed, it heals gently. When resisted, it intensifies. The door of mercy remains open. Grace remains active. Holiness remains possible. And heaven waits—not for perfection achieved alone, but for perfection completed by God.

In Revelation, Jesus rebukes the Church of Laodicea for being neither cold nor hot, warning that such a condition invites rejection rather than approval (Revelation 3:15–16). These words are not spoken to pagans or persecutors. They are spoken to believers who appear religiously alive but are spiritually anesthetized. Lukewarmness is not neutrality. It is not a temporary phase of weakness. It is a condition of divided allegiance in which the heart attempts to belong simultaneously to God and to self. The lukewarm soul does not reject Christ outright, but neither does it surrender fully. It seeks the benefits of faith without the cost of discipleship. It desires heaven without the cross, mercy without repentance, salvation without transformation.

Christ exposes the deception beneath this condition when He says that the lukewarm believe themselves to be rich, prosperous, and in need of nothing, while in reality they are wretched, pitiable, poor, blind, and naked (Revelation 3:17). Lukewarmness is dangerous precisely because it feels safe. Comfort is mistaken for blessing. Stability is mistaken for approval. Familiarity with religious life masks interior poverty. From the beginning, God has demanded the whole heart. Moses commanded Israel to love the Lord with all their heart, soul, and strength (Deuteronomy 6:5). Jesus reaffirmed this as the greatest commandment, adding the mind to the offering of total love (Matthew 22:37). Scripture leaves no space for partial surrender. Love offered in fractions is not love at all.

The prophet Elijah confronted lukewarmness centuries before Christ addressed it in Revelation. Standing before a divided Israel, he asked how long they would limp between two opinions, insisting that if the Lord is God, He must be followed without compromise (1 Kings 18:21). God does not compete for affection. He demands decision. Lukewarmness refuses to decide. Jesus expresses this truth with uncompromising clarity when He teaches that no one can serve two masters, and that devotion to God cannot coexist with attachment to rival loves (Matthew 6:24). Lukewarmness is not limited to wealth. It includes any attachment that negotiates obedience—pride, comfort, reputation, pleasure, control, or fear of human judgment.

One of the most tragic features of lukewarmness is that it often appears virtuous. The lukewarm believer avoids scandalous sin, maintains moral respectability, and often participates actively in religious life. Yet Jesus warns that outward conformity can conceal interior decay. He rebukes those who cleanse the outside while leaving the inside full of disorder, insisting that interior purification must come first (Matthew 23:25–26).

This is why lukewarmness provokes such a strong response from Christ. Coldness can be awakened. Open sin can be confronted. But lukewarmness dulls the conscience. It quiets urgency. It persuades the soul that repentance can wait and that surrender can remain incomplete without consequence. God does not abandon lukewarm souls, but neither does He leave them untouched. The Letter to the Hebrews reminds us that the Lord disciplines those He loves and chastens those He receives as children (Hebrews 12:6). Discipline is not rejection. It is mercy intensified when gentler invitations are ignored. Jesus confirms this when He says plainly that those He loves, He reproves and chastens, calling them not to despair but to zeal and repentance (Revelation 3:19). Chastening is not the opposite of mercy; it is the consequence of mercy refused.

Throughout Scripture, suffering often becomes the instrument by which lukewarm hearts are awakened. The Psalmist confesses that before affliction he went astray, but afterward he kept God's word (Psalm 119:67). Affliction strips away illusion. It dismantles false security. It forces the soul to confront what comfort allowed it to avoid. Jesus warns that lukewarm familiarity with Him does not guarantee entry into His kingdom. He describes a moment when those who ate and drank in His presence and heard Him teach will nevertheless be told that He does not know them because obedience never followed proximity (Luke 13:25–27). Relationship assumed but not cultivated becomes rejection discovered too late. Yet even in this severe warning, mercy remains. Christ does not abandon the lukewarm without first extending an invitation. He stands at the door and knocks, promising intimacy to any who open to Him (Revelation 3:20).

Healing lukewarmness requires decisiveness. Jesus calls not for mild improvement but for zeal—a wholehearted return to obedience. Saint Paul exhorts believers not to be slothful in zeal, but fervent in spirit, serving the Lord (Romans 12:11). Fervency is not perfection. It is direction. It is choosing surrender over negotiation. The fire of God's love is already offered now through grace. This fire purifies without destroying. It heals without condemning. But fire resisted becomes fire endured. The soul must choose whether purification will be embraced freely or experienced through suffering. Saint Peter warns that judgment begins with the household of God (1 Peter 4:17). This judgment is not annihilation, but purification. Lukewarmness delays this work until it becomes unavoidable. This chapter stands as a warning before the narrative turns outward toward tribulation. God will awaken His people. If not through willing surrender, then through refining fire. The choice remains while time remains. Christ's words still echo with urgency: whoever does not bear his cross and follow Him cannot be His disciple (Luke 14:27). Discipleship costs everything—but delay costs more. The fire of love is already burning. Blessed is the soul that runs toward it now, while mercy still invites and grace still transforms.

Lukewarmness does not exhaust God's patience, but it does mark the limit of gentle persuasion. The fire of love that purifies the willing soul quietly does not disappear when it is resisted. It advances. This is not said to frighten, but to clarify. What surrender purifies in one, trial awakens in many. When mercy is ignored at the level of conscience, it is encountered later through consequence.

This is not vengeance. It is intervention.

Scripture reveals that when a people persist in spiritual sleep—when lukewarmness becomes normalized and repentance perpetually delayed—God permits tribulation not to destroy, but to awaken. What purgatory completes in the soul after death, tribulation may confront in the world before death: unfinished conversion, divided allegiance, and forgotten eternity.

Closing Prayer

Eternal Father,

You who search hearts and desire the whole of them,
we bring before You the places within us that remain divided.
Where we have settled for comfort instead of conversion,
where we have lingered in indecision instead of surrender,
have mercy on us.

Expose gently the compromises we have called peace
and the delays we have mistaken for wisdom.

Do not allow us to remain satisfied with partial obedience
or content with faith that costs us nothing. Awaken in us a holy hunger
for You alone.

Where Your fire has approached and we have resisted it,
give us courage to open our hearts now.
Where zeal has faded into routine,
rekindle love that is willing to be purified.
Where fear of loss has restrained obedience,
teach us that only surrender leads to life.

Chasten us only as children You love,
not to wound, but to heal;
not to condemn, but to restore.
Let us recognize discipline as mercy
and correction as invitation.

Grant us the grace to choose decisively while time remains—to run
toward the fire of Your love
rather than meet it later through suffering.
Make us fervent in spirit,
undivided in allegiance,
and ready for the kingdom You prepare.

We ask this in trust, for You desire not our harm, but our holiness.
You do not abandon the lukewarm;
You call them home.

We make this prayer through Christ our Lord.

Amen.

CHAPTER FIVE

THE GREAT TRIBULATION: AWAKENING THROUGH FIRE

THE GREAT TRIBULATION IS OFTEN MISUNDERSTOOD—not as mercy, but as spectacle or threat. Scripture presents it instead as a necessary mercy: a severe but purposeful intervention when gentler invitations have been ignored. Jesus does not introduce tribulation casually. He speaks of it as a time of distress unlike any that has come before, a period so intense that, were it not shortened, no one would survive—but for the sake of the elect, those days will be cut short (Matthew 24:21–22). This alone tells us something crucial: tribulation is not aimed at annihilation, but preservation. Its severity is measured by mercy.

From the beginning, God has used trial not as punishment for its own sake, but as a means of awakening. When Israel wandered from Him, He permitted famine, exile, and oppression—not to destroy the covenant, but to restore it. God allows suffering to interrupt complacency when prosperity has failed to produce obedience. This generation struggles with this truth because it has come to equate love with comfort. Yet Christ never defines love that way. Love pursues the good, not ease. When comfort produces spiritual numbness, love intervenes. Jesus warns that tribulation will come suddenly upon those who assume stability. He compares it to the days of Noah and Lot—times when life appeared normal right up until judgment fell (Luke 17:26–30). People were eating, drinking, buying, selling, planting, and building. Nothing seemed urgent. Nothing seemed wrong. That normalcy was itself the danger.

Tribulation is God's interruption of false normal.

The prophet Amos records God asking a piercing question: if disaster comes to a city, has the Lord not done it? (Amos 3:6). This is not a declaration of cruelty, but of sovereignty. God is not a passive observer of history. When moral decay becomes systemic and repentance is persistently resisted, God permits consequences that expose truth. The Great Tribulation, then, is not primarily about persecution from without, but revelation from within. It unmasks what has been hidden. Jesus says it will be a time when lawlessness increases and the love of many grows cold (Matthew 24:12). What tribulation reveals is not merely suffering, but spiritual condition. This is why Scripture repeatedly warns believers—not unbelievers—to remain vigilant. Judgment, Peter tells us, begins with the household of God (1 Peter 4:17). Tribulation is not directed first at atheists, but at a Church tempted toward comfort without conversion. Yet even here, mercy dominates. Jesus assures that those who endure to the end will be saved (Matthew 24:13). Endurance is not survival alone; it is fidelity. Tribulation strips away illusions so that genuine faith can stand revealed. What cannot endure fire was never built on truth.

Revelation depicts tribulation in terrifying imagery, yet always to call for repentance. Even after severe judgments, many refused to repent (Revelation 9:20–21). This refusal reveals the deepest tragedy—not suffering itself, but hearts that remain hardened even when mercy takes the form of warning. Yet Scripture does not leave tribulation suspended in despair; it frames it within a larger movement toward renewal. Jesus Himself describes tribulation as birth pangs (Matthew 24:8). Birth pangs are painful, but they signal life, not death. They announce that something new is coming into being. Tribulation, rightly understood, is not the end of God's plan, but the painful labor that gives way to renewal. This is why Saint John speaks of saints who emerge from tribulation in his vision (Revelation 7:9–10). Not everyone awakens, but some do. Those who respond to tribulation with repentance, humility, and faith emerge refined rather than destroyed. Daniel records that many shall purify themselves and make themselves white and be refined, while the wicked shall act wickedly still (Daniel 12:10). Fire reveals difference. The question tribulation forces upon every soul is the same question grace has always asked: Who do you serve? When comforts collapse, allegiances are revealed. When security fails, foundations are exposed. What was lukewarm is forced to choose. Tribulation is not inevitable, but conditional. God delays judgment in patience, desiring repentance (2 Peter 3:9); when patience is exhausted, consequence follows.

This chapter is not written to incite fear, but to restore seriousness. Tribulation is not God losing control; it is God asserting truth. It is mercy refusing to allow sleep to become permanent. The same Christ who warns of tribulation also promises presence. He assures His followers that He will be with them always, even to the close of the age (Matthew 28:20). Tribulation is not abandonment. It is accompaniment under pressure. For the awakened soul, tribulation is not terror—it is confirmation. For the lukewarm, it is invitation sharpened by necessity. For those asleep, it is the alarm that cannot be ignored. God does not delight in shaking the world. But when the world refuses to awaken, shaking becomes mercy. The fire comes not to consume what belongs to God, but to reveal it. When the shaking subsides—whether in life or at the hour of death—what remains is not what we intended, claimed, or planned to do for God, but what was actually offered to Him in love. Scripture is unwavering on this point: every work will be tested, not by appearance, but by truth. What was built for God endures. What was built for self, even if religious in form, does not. Every awakening leaves the soul with a quiet reckoning: what of my life was truly given to God?

The tragedy Scripture warns against is not merely sin forgiven, but purpose wasted. Purification may reveal that much of what filled our lives bore no enduring weight before God. The fire that awakens also evaluates. It does not only purify the soul; it reveals the worth of what the soul has offered. God's mercy is generous, but it is not sentimental. Love desires communion, but truth demands reckoning. What is not surrendered to God cannot be carried into eternity. What is not rooted in love does not last.

Closing Prayer

Elohim and Adonai,

You who govern all things in truth and mercy,
teach us to recognize Your hand even when it comes through fire.

25

Where comfort has made us careless, awaken us.
Where stability has dulled our love, unsettle us gently.
Where illusion has replaced obedience, strip it away.
Do not allow us to mistake calm for faith
or normalcy for holiness.

If trial must come, grant us endurance.
If shaking must occur, let it reveal what is true.
If fire must pass through our lives,
let it refine rather than destroy.
Preserve in us what belongs to You,
and burn away what cannot endure Your presence.

Keep our hearts from hardening when mercy speaks loudly.
Give us eyes to see tribulation not as abandonment,
but as invitation sharpened by urgency.
Teach us to respond with repentance rather than resistance,
with humility rather than fear.

Remain with us, Lord, as You have promised.
Stand beside those who endure,
strengthen those who awaken,
and draw to Yourself those who are willing to be made new.

When all false securities fall away,
let what remains be faith rooted in love,
obedience shaped by truth,
and lives offered wholly to You.

We place ourselves in Your hands—
not asking for ease,
but for faithfulness.

We ask this through Christ our Lord.

Amen.

CHAPTER SIX
WHAT ENDURES BEFORE GOD

T HERE COMES A MOMENT—SOMETIMES AFTER suffering, sometimes after loss, sometimes simply in stillness—when the noise fades and the soul is left alone with a single question: What was it all finally for? Scripture insists that this moment is not optional. It comes to every life. Whether gently or abruptly, whether welcomed or resisted, the day arrives when everything we have done is seen for what it is. Not what it looked like. Not what we intended. But what it truly was.

Jesus speaks of this moment with quiet clarity when He warns that treasures laid up on earth are vulnerable to decay and loss, while treasures laid up in heaven endure. Where one's treasure is, He says, there the heart will also be (Matthew 6:19–21). The point is not merely moral exhortation, but revelation. What lasts is shown to be what was ordered toward God. What fades is what was gathered without reference to Him. This is not primarily a punishment, but a disclosure. It tells the truth. What is lost, then, is not the soul that belongs to God, but the weightless pursuits to which time, affection, and energy were given without eternal direction. Scripture never says that everything we do is evil. It says that everything not rooted in love does not last. This truth is difficult for a generation accustomed to measuring life by productivity, recognition, and achievement. We are trained to ask what we accomplished, what we built, what we accumulated. Yet the deeper question is not simply what was done, but for whom it was done.

Jesus tells a story of servants entrusted with resources while their master is away. Some invest what they are given and return it with increase. One hides what he received, returning it untouched. The master's judgment is not based on effort alone, but on fidelity. What was entrusted was meant to be offered back in love (Matthew 25:14–30). The tragedy is not that the servant failed spectacularly. It is that he preserved what was given without offering it. Neutrality, Christ reveals, is not safe. What is not given is lost. This is why Jesus warns that even acts that appear religious can be empty. He speaks of those who pray, fast, and give alms for human recognition. Their actions are not condemned as immoral, but as misplaced. "They have received their reward," He says plainly (Matthew 6:2). The work was done, but not for God. And so its reward does not pass beyond time.

This is a sobering realization: good things done for the wrong end do not endure.

The contemplative heart begins to see how much of life is lived in fragments—some moments offered to God, others guarded for self. Prayer given quickly. Charity offered when convenient. Obedience negotiated. Faith compartmentalized. None of this feels dramatic. It feels normal. But Scripture quietly insists that eternity does not measure normality. It measures love. Saint Paul writes that if he speaks in the tongues of men and angels, has prophetic power, understands mysteries, and possesses faith strong enough to move mountains—but lacks love—he gains nothing (1 Corinthians 13:1–3). Nothing. The word is devastating in its simplicity. Without love, even spiritual greatness evaporates.

What is love, then, in this context? It is not feeling. It is not intention. Love is the ordering of the will toward God. It is choosing Him not only in prayer, but in decision. Not only in belief, but in surrender. Jesus makes this unmistakably clear when He says that whoever wishes to save his life will lose it, but whoever loses his life for His sake will find it (Matthew 16:25). What is held tightly for self dissolves. What is offered freely to God endures.

This chapter is contemplative because it asks the reader to look honestly at their own life—not in panic, but in truth. Where were my days spent? What did I love most? What did I protect from God? What did I give Him only partially? The answers are not meant to condemn; they are meant to clarify. Saint Paul speaks of suffering loss even while being saved, "yet so as through fire" (1 Corinthians 3:15). Something remains. Something is lost.

What is lost is what was never surrendered. This is why the saints lived with such intentionality. Not urgency driven by fear, but focus driven by love. Saint Paul confesses that he presses on toward the goal, forgetting what lies behind and straining forward to what lies ahead (Philippians 3:13–14). His life is not frantic. It is ordered. This generation often imagines that God will sort everything out later. Scripture agrees—but not in the way we assume. God does not retroactively infuse love into what was lived without Him. He reveals it. He completes what was offered. He releases what was withheld.

This is not harsh. It is honest.

When Jesus speaks of judgment, He does not describe a courtroom obsessed with rule-keeping. He describes a revelation of love. "As you did it to one of the least of these my brethren, you did it to me" (Matthew 25:40). What mattered was not visibility, but intention. Not scale, but surrender. The contemplative soul begins to understand that eternity is not built at the end of life. It is built daily, quietly and repeatedly. In ordinary choices offered to God. Nothing done in love is wasted, nothing withheld from God survives. This is the freedom hidden within this sobering truth. When we give our lives to God—not perfectly, but sincerely—nothing is lost. Even suffering is redeemed. Even failure is healed. What is lost is only what we refused to give.

The invitation, then, is not to despair over what has passed, but to consecrate what remains. Saint John assures us that if we walk in the light, the blood of Jesus cleanses us from all sin (1 John 1:7). What can still be offered can still be purified. What can still be surrendered can still endure. The final measure of a life is not how much was done, but how much was given.

All not done for God is lost.
But all done for God—no matter how small—remains forever.

Closing Prayer

Eternal God,

Before whom nothing is hidden

31

and in whose light all things are revealed,
teach us to desire what endures.

When our lives are weighed—not by appearance,
not by success, not by intention alone— but by love,
have mercy on what we have guarded for ourselves
and receive what we have offered to You.

Purify our motives where they have been mixed,
heal our attachments where they have been divided,
and gently release us from what cannot last.
Do not allow us to cling to what time will take away,
but draw our hearts toward what remains in You.

Where we have given only partially,
invite us into fuller surrender.
Where we have lived distracted,
restore holy attention.
Where love has been small but sincere,
let nothing be lost.

Teach us to live deliberately—
not driven by fear,
but ordered by love;
not frantic, but faithful.

Consecrate what remains of our days,
that each ordinary moment
may be offered back to You.
Let what we do be done for You,
with You, and in You.

When all is finally revealed,
may we discover not a life wasted,
but a life given.

We place what has been
and what still may be
into Your hands, trusting that nothing offered in love is ever lost.

Through Christ our Lord.

Amen.

CHAPTER SEVEN

WHEN GRACE IS REJECTED

NOT EVERYONE WILL BE SANCTIFIED. This sentence is difficult, but Scripture does not avoid it. God offers grace to all. He desires that all be saved. He patiently invites, corrects, purifies, and waits. Yet love, if it is real, does not coerce. Sanctification must be received. Grace must be accepted. And Scripture is clear that some will refuse—freely, persistently, and finally.

Hell is not the failure of God's mercy. It is the consequence of its rejection. God's mercy does not cease with resistance; it pursues the human soul to the very end of earthly life. Jesus spoke of hell more than anyone else in Scripture—not to terrify, but to tell the truth. He did not speculate, exaggerate, or threaten. He spoke of it as a real and final possibility. He warned that the gate is wide and the way easy that leads to destruction, and many enter by it, while the gate is narrow and the way hard that leads to life, and few find it (Matthew 7:13–14). These words are not speculative; they are diagnostic. Hell is not imposed on souls who desire God but fall short. That is the error many make when imagining divine judgment. Purgatory exists precisely because God does not abandon imperfect souls who love Him. Hell, by contrast, is the end chosen by those who will not be healed—who refuse sanctification itself. Jesus names this principle plainly: whoever loves his life loses it, and whoever relinquishes his life in this world keeps it for eternal life (John 12:25). Love turned inward collapses; love turned toward God opens into life. Hell is the final inward collapse of a will that refuses communion and not the fate of those who sought God and failed in weakness. The Gospel shows Jesus forgiving repentant sinners again and again—tax collectors, adulterers, thieves, the violent. What excludes is not weakness, but refusal. Jesus warns that blasphemy against the Holy Spirit will not be forgiven (Matthew 12:31). This is not a single utterance, but a settled resistance to grace—the persistent rejection of the very means by which forgiveness is received. This is why the reality of hell cannot be separated from the call to sanctification. Sanctification is not an optional spiritual upgrade. It is the process by which the soul becomes capable of communion with God. To reject sanctification is to reject heaven itself. Scripture states plainly that without holiness no one will see the Lord (Hebrews 12:14). Holiness is not moral perfection achieved alone; it is cooperation with grace. But cooperation must occur.

Jesus describes judgment not first in terms of fire, but in terms of separation. "Depart from me," He says (Matthew 7:23). The terror lies in distance, not punishment. Hell is the final state of a soul that no longer desires communion. This separation is not imposed arbitrarily. Scripture consistently presents it as chosen, emphasizing that judgment corresponds to desire. Jesus weeps over Jerusalem not because they were weak, but because they were unwilling: "O Jerusalem, Jerusalem, killing the prophets and stoning those who are sent to you! How often would I have gathered your children together as a hen gathers her brood under her wings, and you would not!" (Matthew 23:37). Grace was extended. Mercy was present. But it was refused. This refusal can take many forms. Some reject God openly. Others do so quietly, persistently, through delay, rationalization, or self rule. Hell is not reserved only for the violent or the infamous. Jesus warns that many who say "Lord, Lord" will not enter the kingdom, because obedience never followed belief (Matthew 7:21). Familiarity with God is not the same as surrender to Him.

Scripture describes hell as the place prepared for the devil and his angels (Matthew 25:41). This is important. Hell was not created as a destination for humanity. It becomes one only when human beings align their will permanently against God, choosing self over sacrifice, autonomy over communion, darkness over light. Jesus uses strong imagery to convey this reality—not to indulge imagination, but to awaken conscience. He speaks of outer darkness, where there is weeping and gnashing of teeth (Matthew 8:12). Darkness signifies separation from God, who is light. Weeping signifies loss. Gnashing of teeth signifies hardened resistance, not repentance. Hell is not remorse seeking mercy; it is refusal hardened into permanence. In hell it is judgment rather than purification. Hebrews tells us that it is appointed for human beings to die once, and after that comes judgment (Hebrews 9:27). Choice belongs to time. Eternity reveals the consequence of that choice.

Modern discomfort with hell often stems from a misunderstanding of love. We imagine love as unconditional affirmation. The Gospel reveals love as truth-filled communion. God does not force Himself on those who do not want Him. To do so would violate the very dignity He bestowed. C. S. Lewis captured this truth succinctly: in the end, there are only two kinds of people—those who say to God, "Thy will be done," and those to whom God says, "Thy will be done." Jesus' most sobering parable on judgment is the separation of the sheep and the goats (Matthew 25:31–46). The division is not based on belief statements, but on love embodied—or withheld. Those who loved Christ in the least were drawn into the kingdom. Those who refused love excluded themselves. The final judgment reveals not intentions, but decisions. Hell, then, is not God losing control. It is God honoring human freedom to its ultimate end.

This chapter must be read carefully. The reality of hell is not presented to produce despair, but seriousness. Jesus never spoke of hell to those who were humbly seeking God. He spoke of it to those who presumed upon grace, who mistook patience for permission, who believed that delay carried no consequence. Those asleep often imagine that everyone will eventually be saved simply because God is good. Scripture never teaches this. It teaches instead that God is good and just, merciful and truthful. Love does not negate consequence; it explains it. Hell is the final tragedy not because God desires it, but because some souls do. The prophet Ezekiel records God's own heart when He says that He takes no pleasure in the death of the wicked, but desires that they turn from their ways and live (Ezekiel 33:11). The offer stands. But it can be refused. This truth gives urgency to everything that precedes it. Delay matters. Lukewarmness matters. Resistance matters. What is postponed long enough can become rejected entirely. Sanctification refused does not become purgatory by default. Purgatory completes love unfinished; hell confirms love rejected. Yet even here, the chapter does not end in despair. It ends in clarity.

As long as life remains, grace remains. As long as the heart can still respond, sanctification is still possible. Scripture assures us that God is

37

patient, not wishing that any should perish, but that all should reach repentance (2 Peter 3:9). The tragedy of hell is not that mercy was absent, but that it was refused. This chapter stands as a warning—not because God delights in punishment, but because truth demands honesty. Love invites. Love waits. Love purifies. But love also allows rejection.

And that is why the call to awaken is not optional.

Eternity does not negotiate.
Grace does not compel.
Love does not lie.

The reality of hell is the final proof that our choices matter—now, not later.

This truth inevitably raises a question that cannot be avoided. If hell is real, if grace can be refused, and if sanctification must be received rather than assumed, then assurance itself must be examined honestly. What does it mean to belong to God? How can one know whether grace has truly been received—or merely presumed? And if salvation is offered freely, what role does cooperation, perseverance, and response actually play? These are not abstract questions reserved for theologians. They arise naturally when eternity is taken seriously. Some live in quiet fear, uncertain whether they are saved despite their desire to love God. Others live in false confidence, convinced of salvation while resisting conversion. Still others oscillate between trust and anxiety, sincerity and delay. The danger lies not only in rejection, but also in misunderstanding.

The next chapter turns toward this question directly—not to unsettle tender consciences, nor to offer easy reassurance, but to speak truthfully about assurance, presumption, and the nature of salvation itself. If grace can be refused, then it must also be rightly received. And if salvation is God's work, then it must be understood on God's terms, not our assumptions. Only in that clarity can hope be real.

Closing Prayer

Merciful and Just God,

You who desire that none be lost
and who never cease to invite,
we stand before You aware of the seriousness of our freedom.

Keep us from presuming upon Your grace
as though love required no response
and mercy carried no consequence.
Deliver us from the quiet refusal
that hides behind delay, rationalization, or self-rule.

Where our hearts have resisted healing,
soften them.
Where we have mistaken patience for permission,
restore reverence.
Where we have spoken Your name without surrendering our will,
teach us what it means to belong to You.

Do not allow us to choose distance
when communion is offered.
Do not allow fear to harden us,
nor comfort to numb us.
Grant us the grace to desire holiness,
not as burden,
but as the only path to life with You.

As long as breath remains in us,
keep the door of repentance open.
Give us courage to receive grace fully,
to cooperate with sanctification willingly,
and to say yes while yes is still possible.

Let us never reject what You patiently extend,
nor refuse the love that seeks to heal us.

39

Teach us to say with honesty and trust:
Your will be done— not only with our lips,
but with our lives. We place our freedom into Your hands,
confident not in ourselves,
but in Your truth and Your mercy.

Through Christ our Lord.

Amen.

CHAPTER EIGHT
CAN I LOSE MY SALVATION?

THE QUESTION IS OFTEN ASKED QUIETLY, sometimes anxiously, and sometimes with misplaced confidence: "If I am saved—and if I consider myself awake—can I lose my salvation?"

Salvation, in the Christian vision, is not a static possession stored away for later use. It is a living relationship, sustained by grace, received through faith, and perfected through love. Whether salvation can be lost depends not on God's faithfulness—Scripture is unwavering on that—but on how the human will responds to grace over time. The New Testament never presents salvation as fragile in God's hands. But it also never presents it as automatic, mechanical, or immune to refusal. The tension exists because salvation involves both divine initiative and human cooperation. Grace is given freely. It must also be received freely. Christian tradition has long recognized that souls do not stand before God in the same interior posture, and that questions of assurance, perseverance, and loss cannot be answered without first discerning the condition of the heart. What follows are four such states—not as labels for condemnation, but as mirrors for discernment.

1. Souls Learning to Rest in Mercy

There are those who are saved but do not yet know it. They love God sincerely, desire to please Him, and grieve over sin, yet live under a persistent cloud of doubt. They struggle with despair—not despair of God's goodness, but despair of themselves. They believe, often unconsciously, that salvation depends on their performance rather than on Christ's work. These souls are marked by effort more than rest, vigilance more than joy. They pray faithfully, repent often, and strive to obey—but lack assurance. They fear presumption so much that they drift toward self reliance. Grace is acknowledged, but not fully trusted. Scripture speaks gently to such souls. Saint John writes that perfect love casts out fear, and that fear has to do with punishment (1 John 4:18). God does not desire His children to live in constant dread. Jesus Himself invites the weary to rest, not to perform more efficiently (Matthew 11:28).

Their struggle is not rebellion, but misunderstanding. Their doubt does not come from resistance to grace, but from an incomplete grasp of it. God deals tenderly with such hearts. Through patience, formation, and deeper trust, He brings them—slowly and faithfully (with their cooperation)—into assurance. God teaches them that salvation is not earned but received. Their journey is one of illumination, not exclusion. What they lack is not salvation, but confidence in God's mercy. They do not lose salvation. They grow into knowing they are saved.

2. Assured by the Spirit

These are those who are saved and know it—not because of pride, but because the Holy Spirit bears witness within them. Saint Paul describes this confidence when he writes that the Spirit Himself bears witness with our spirit that we are children of God (Romans 8:16). This is not presumption. It is filial assurance. These souls do not claim salvation because of their moral performance. They know their weakness. They know their need for mercy. But they also know, deeply and quietly, that they belong to God. Their confidence is rooted not in themselves, but in Christ. They love God, fear Him rightly, repent sincerely, and desire holiness. When they fall, they return quickly. When they sin, they grieve. When they obey, they give thanks.

God does not abandon what He begins. Salvation is not sustained by human strength alone, but by divine faithfulness. However, this promise does not eliminate cooperation. God completes His work with the willing soul, not apart from it. Where cooperation is imperfect—and it always is—purification may be required. But purification presupposes love. For such souls, if sanctification remains incomplete at death, God completes it through mercy. What is not finished on earth is not discarded, but refined. They do not lose salvation, but are drawn onward into its fullness.

3. Confidence Without Conversion

This is the most dangerous category—not because God's mercy is absent, but because it is presumed upon. These are those who believe they are saved regardless of how they live. Grace is treated as a safety net rather than a transforming power. There is little remorse for sin, little reverence for God, and little desire for holiness. This posture often hides behind familiar phrases: "God understands." "God is love." "Once saved, always saved." These statements can be true in the right context, but here they are emptied of meaning. Grace becomes permission. Mercy becomes entitlement. Repentance becomes optional.

Scripture speaks directly to this danger. Saint Paul warns that we must not continue in sin so that grace may abound (Romans 6:1). Grace does not excuse sin; it frees us from it. Jesus warns that not everyone who calls Him "Lord" will enter the kingdom, but only those who do the will of His Father (Matthew 7:21).

Salvation is not mere belief. It is not verbal profession. It is not familiarity with religious language. It is union with Christ—a union that transforms the will. Where there is no repentance, no reverence, and no desire for holiness, there is no saving relationship. These souls may be convinced they are saved. They may even be confident. But confidence is not assurance. Presumption is not faith. To treat grace as a license to remain unchanged is to reject grace itself. Such souls do not lose salvation; rather, if unrepentant, they discover—painfully, at the end—that it was never received.

4. The Will Set Against Grace

Finally, there are those who are not saved and know it—and are content with that fact. They have heard the Word. The seed was sown. But their hearts are hardened. Scripture describes this condition when it speaks of the enemy coming to steal the Word away before it can take root

(Matthew 13:19). These souls question God's sovereignty, goodness, and authority. They resist reverence. They dismiss accountability. Their rejection is not confused; it is chosen. Over time, indifference hardens into resistance. Scripture does not present this state lightly. Hebrews warns that the heart can become hardened through the deceitfulness of sin (Hebrews 3:13). Rejection repeated becomes rejection fixed. Persistent resistance to grace renders the soul deaf to its call. And in the end, they receive what they have chosen. God does not force salvation on the unwilling. Love does not compel. Judgment, in this case, is not arbitrary punishment, but the honoring of freedom exercised without repentance.

So, the conclusion is this: loss applies only where something has first been truly received. The real question is not whether salvation can be lost, but whether it was ever received in the first place. The danger lies not in losing salvation, but in presuming upon grace. God does not abandon those brought into the life of faith in Jesus Christ, for the saving work of Christ is complete, enduring and cannot be undone. What varies is not God's constancy, but the heart's openness to grace.

Here is the good news, the most important truth of all: **salvation is still being offered today.**

As long as life remains, mercy remains. As long as the heart can still respond, grace is still extended. Scripture assures us that God desires all to be saved and to come to the knowledge of the truth (1 Timothy 2:4). The door closes only when the will insists on keeping it shut. This chapter is not meant to provoke fear, but clarity. Salvation is not fragile in God's hands—but it is not automatic in ours. Grace is a gift, not a guarantee without response. Love invites, waits, and purifies. It does not deceive.

If you are awake, remain watchful. If you are uncertain, trust more deeply. If you have presumed, repent quickly. If you have resisted, return while you still can. Today, the invitation still stands. Mercy is still offered. Grace is still sufficient. And the call to awaken has not been withdrawn.

A Note on Christian Tradition

The distinctions described in this chapter do not propose a new doctrine, nor do they attempt to resolve every mystery surrounding salvation. Rather, they reflect a long-

44

standing Christian approach to spiritual discernment—one that recognizes differing interior dispositions toward grace, repentance, and perseverance.

Throughout Scripture and the Church's spiritual tradition, careful attention has been given to the difference between weakness and refusal, between humble trust and presumption, and between salvation received and salvation resisted. These distinctions have served not to unsettle sincere souls, but to awaken conscience, correct false confidence, and lead hearts more fully into truth.

This chapter follows that pastoral tradition. Its purpose is not to classify persons, but to clarify postures of the heart, so that grace may be welcomed rightly, mercy trusted honestly, and response made without delay.

Closing Prayer

Faithful God,

You who do not revoke Your gifts in Christ,
and who never abandon what You begin,
we place our hearts before You in truth.

Free us from fear that doubts Your mercy
and from confidence that presumes upon it.
Where we have struggled with assurance,
teach us to rest in what Christ has accomplished.
Where we have mistaken familiarity for communion,
call us back to repentance and reverence.

Give us hearts that receive grace fully—
not resisting its demand to transform,
not softening its call to holiness.
Let us neither despair of salvation
nor treat it lightly.

Where we are sincere but uncertain,
speak peace.
Where we are confident but unchanged,
awaken us.
Where we have delayed response,
grant urgency.
Where we have resisted,
grant humility to return.

Teach us to cooperate with grace
day by day, to persevere in faith,
to walk in the light,
and to desire sanctification not as burden
but as belonging.

As long as life remains,
keep our hearts open.
As long as mercy is offered,
give us the courage to receive it.
Let us never close the door
You continue to hold open.

We entrust ourselves not to our own strength,
but to Your faithfulness—
confident that what is received in love
will be brought to completion by You.

Through Jesus Christ our Lord.

Amen.

CONCLUSION
AWAKE, AND WALK IN THE LIGHT

I F THIS BOOK HAS DONE ITS WORK, it has not left you afraid. It has left you awake. True awakening brings clarity, not anxiety. Anxiety scatters the soul. Awakening gathers it. Anxiety looks for escape. Awakening looks for truth. Scripture never calls us to panic about eternity; it calls us to live in its light. Saint Paul speaks of this light when he writes that the night is far gone and the day is at hand, urging believers to cast off the works of darkness and put on the armor of light (Romans 13:12). Light does not threaten what belongs to it. It clarifies, orders, and reveals the path forward. What has been uncovered in these pages is not a cruel reality, but an honest one: God takes our lives seriously because He loves us deeply. He does not rush the soul, but He does not flatter it either. Mercy invites. Truth completes. Love finishes what grace begins.

The sleeping generation is not condemned for having slept. Sleep is human. What matters is waking. Scripture assures us that awakening is always possible while time remains. Jesus Himself says that whoever comes to Him He will not cast out (John 6:37). That promise is not conditional on perfection, but on sincerity. God does not wait for flawless souls; He waits for willing ones. Hope, then, does not rest on our ability to purify ourselves completely. It rests on God's faithfulness to complete what He has begun. The burden of perfection does not fall on us alone. The responsibility of response does.

This is where the book leaves you—not with a checklist, but with a posture. The path forward is not heroic effort, but honest cooperation. Saint Paul does not ask us to outrun grace. He asks us to walk with it. "If we live by the Spirit, let us also walk by the Spirit" (Galatians 5:25). Walking implies steadiness, not frenzy. Direction, not drama. Awakening reshapes ordinary life. It does not remove us from the world; it reorders how we inhabit it. Work becomes offering. Suffering becomes participation. Love becomes intention. Even failure, when surrendered, becomes material for mercy. Jesus does not send awakened disciples into hiding. He sends them into the world—not to dominate it, but to illuminate it. "You are the light of the world," He says, not as flattery, but as responsibility (Matthew 5:14). Light does not draw attention to itself. It makes other things visible.

This is the sending.

To live awake in a sleeping world is not to shout, but to remain faithful. Not to predict judgment, but to embody truth. Not to only condemn darkness, but to refuse to cooperate with it. Saint Peter exhorts believers to live honorably so that even those who oppose them may see their good deeds and glorify God (1 Peter 2:12). Hope is not optimism about outcomes; it is trust in God's character. Even in tribulation, even in purification, even in loss, Scripture assures us that God works all things together for good for those who love Him (Romans 8:28). Good does not always mean comfortable. It always means redemptive.

The final word of this book is not fire. It is faithfulness.

Not urgency divorced from peace, but urgency rooted in love. Not fear of loss, but desire for fullness. Not withdrawal from the world, but deeper engagement with it—on God's terms. Jesus' final instruction to His disciples was not a warning, but a promise. He told them to go, to teach, to baptize, to live the truth—and then He said, "I am with you always, to the close of the age" (Matthew 28:20). God does not send without accompanying.

If you are awake now, do not rush to do more. Begin by loving more honestly. Pray more attentively. Repent more freely. Forgive more quickly. Offer more intentionally. None of these are grand gestures. They are eternal ones.

Nothing done for God is lost.
Nothing offered in love is wasted.
Nothing surrendered is forgotten.

The night is far gone. The day is at hand. Walk in the light.

Closing Benediction

May the God who awakens the sleeper
grant you light where there has been delay,
clarity where there has been confusion,
and courage where there has been hesitation.

May Christ, who calls gently yet truthfully,
draw your heart fully to Himself,
complete what grace has begun,
and teach you to love without reserve.

May the Holy Spirit keep you attentive to eternity,
faithful in small obediences,
patient in purification,
and steadfast in hope.

May your life be offered freely,
your love be given honestly,
and your days be lived awake.

And when the night finally gives way to morning,
may you be found ready—not by fear, but by love.

Amen.

SCRIPTURAL PATHWAYS

A Guide to the Sacred Texts Referenced in This Work

The following passages of Sacred Scripture appear throughout this book. They are presented here not merely as references, but as threads woven through the call to vigilance, sanctification, and hope. Readers are encouraged to return to these texts prayerfully, allowing the Word of God to continue its work beyond the page.

The Call to Awakening and Vigilance

Romans
13:11–12

Ephesians
5:14

Matthew
24:37–42
25:1–13

Luke
19:42

Delay, Obedience, and the Urgency of Response

Proverbs
27:1

James
4:14

Hebrews
3:13–15

Joshua
24:15

Holiness, Purification, and Readiness for Heaven

Hebrews
12:14

Isaiah
6:3–7

Malachi
3:2–3

1 Corinthians
3:12–15

Revelation
21:27

Mercy, Forgiveness, and Interior Transformation

1 John
1:7
1:9
3:2–3

Philippians
1:6
2:12–13

Psalm
119:67

Lukewarmness, Division of Heart, and the Fire of Love

Revelation
3:15–20

1 Kings
18:21

Matthew
6:24
23:25–26

Romans
12:11

Tribulation, Refinement, and Awakening Through Trial

Matthew
24:8
24:21–22

Daniel
12:10

Revelation
7:9–10
9:20–21

1 Peter
4:17

Judgment, Freedom, and the Reality of Choice

Matthew
7:13–14
7:21–23
25:31–46

Luke
13:25–27

Hebrews
9:27

Ezekiel
33:11

Salvation, Assurance, and Cooperation with Grace

Romans
8:16

John
12:25

Philippians
3:12–14

1 Timothy
2:4

What Endures Before God

Matthew
6:19–21

Matthew
25:14–30

1 Corinthians
13:1–3

Matthew
25:40

ABOUT THE PUBLISHER

Quiet Watch Publishing was founded to serve readers seeking depth, reverence, and spiritual clarity in an age marked by distraction and haste. Its mission is to publish works that call the Christian soul to vigilance, interior honesty, and faithful response to grace—without sensationalism, polemic, or dilution of truth.

The titles released under Quiet Watch Publishing are intentionally contemplative in nature. They are written not for hurried consumption, but for careful reading, prayerful reflection, and sustained engagement. Drawing from Sacred Scripture and the historic Christian tradition, these works aim to restore seriousness to questions often treated casually, and hope to themes frequently reduced to sentiment.

Quiet Watch Publishing operates quietly by design. Its focus is not on authorial prominence or cultural relevance, but on fidelity—to the Gospel, to the Church's wisdom, and to the dignity of the reader's conscience. The press exists to support works that invite conversion rather than comfort, depth rather than distraction, and truth spoken in charity rather than fear.